Swimming Is Fun!

by Robin Nelson

first step nonfiction

Lerner Publications Company · Minneapolis

The images in this book are used with the permission of: © iStockphoto.com/Anton Balazh, p. 4; © Christopher Futcher/Vetta/Getty Images, p. 5; © iStockphoto.com/kali9, p. 6; © iStockphoto.com/ William Britten, p. 7; © iStockphoto.com/brocreative, p. 8; © iStockphoto.com/Tetiana Zbrodko, p. 9; © iStockphoto.com/mamahoohooba, p. 10; © iStockphoto.com/1MoreCreative, p. 11; © Suzanne Tucker/Shutterstock.com, p. 12; © iStockphoto.com/Jason Titzer, pp. 13, 15; © iStockphoto.com/Rayna Januska, p. 14, 17; © Andreykuzmin/Dreamstime.com, p. 16; © iStockphoto.com/emmgunn, p. 18; © iStockphoto.com/Christopher Futcher, p. 19; © Laura Westlund/Independent Picture Service, p. 21.

Front cover: © Datacraft Co Ltd/Getty Images.

Main body text set in ITC Avant Garde Gothic Std Medium 21/25.
Typeface provided by Adobe Systems.

Lerner Publications Company
A division of Lerner Publishing Group, Inc.
241 First Avenue North
Minneapolis, MN 55401 U.S.A.

Website address: www.lernerbooks.com

Library of Congress Cataloging-in-Publication Data

Nelson, Robin, 1971–
    Swimming is fun! / by Robin Nelson.
        p.   cm. — (First step nonfiction—sports are fun!)
    Includes index.
    ISBN 978–1–4677–1106–7 (lib. bdg. : alk. paper)
    ISBN 978–1–4677–1748–9 (eBook)
    1. Swimming—Juvenile literature. I. Title.
GV837.6.N45 2014
797.2'1—dc23   2012044594

Manufactured in the United States of America
1 – PC – 7/15/13

Table of Contents

Do you like to swim?

You can swim for fun or be on a team.

Swim teams have coaches.

Coaches help their team swim faster.

A swimmer wears a swimsuit.

Swimmers wear **goggles** to keep water out of their eyes.

Swimmers often wear a **swim cap** to keep their hair out of the way.

A swim cap helps you move through the water faster.

Swim teams race other teams at a swim **meet**.

Your race is called your **event**.

Each event uses different
strokes.

The breaststroke is the slowest stroke.

The crawl is the fastest stroke.

The butterfly pushes you
above the water.

You swim the backstroke on your back.

Swimming is fun!

The Pool

At a swim meet, the pool is divided into lanes. Swimmers stand on starting blocks. They dive into their lanes. At the end of their race, they touch the timing pad. It records their time.

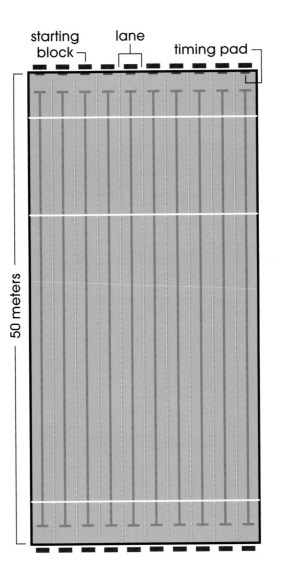

starting block

lane

timing pad

50 meters

Fun Facts

- Swimming is a great way to get in shape. It uses most of the body's muscles.

- In some events, swimmers swim one length of the pool. In other events, they swim back and forth many times.

- In a relay event, four swimmers are on a team. Each swimmer swims a different stroke.

Glossary

event – a race in a swim meet

goggles – special eye coverings that swimmers wear to keep water out of their eyes

meet – a swimming competition

strokes – styles of swimming

swim cap – a covering that stretches over a swimmer's hair

Index